The Art of Reading Gestures & Postures

BODY
Language

Vinay Mohan Sharma

V&S PUBLISHERS

Published by

V&S PUBLISHERS

F-2/16, Ansari Road, Daryaganj, New Delhi-110002
☎ 011-23240026, 011-23240027 • *Fax* 011-23240028
Email info@vspublishers.com • *Website* www.vspublishers.com

Regional Office Hyderabad
5-1-707/1, Brij Bhawan (Beside Central Bank of India Lane)
Bank Street, Koti, Hyderabad - 500 095
☎ 040-24737290
E-mail vspublishershyd@gmail.com

Branch Office Mumbai
Godown # 34 at The Model Co-Operative Housing, Society Ltd.,
"Sahakar Niwas", Ground Floor, Next to Sobo Central, Mumbai - 400 034
☎ 022-23510736
E-mail vspublishersmum@gmail.com

Follow us on 🇹 🇫 in

All books available at **www.vspublishers.com**

Printed at Param Offseters Okhla New Delhi-110020

Contents

Preface

When we speak something, it is our body and its gestures that help in conveying the desired message effectively and easily. Sometimes we don't utter a single word, and yet we are able to communicate a lot. It is because our body parts, especially our facial expressions combined with various other gestures, speak a language of their own, which we call body language. It is not always that what we speak is really what we intend to say. Most of the time, while speaking, we do actually act. Our acting involves varying our speech and body gestures to suit different circumstances which we come across on different occasions in our daily life.

The whole world is like a stage where we all are mere performers. That is why we talk and behave differently with different people. While living in the same environment with a similar set of people for long, one tends to become stereotyped in one's behaviour. And, in that case, it is highly possible that our acquaintances or people who interact with us regularly can easily understand our body language. Frankly speaking, body language is the only language which is common all over the world. Everybody can easily communicate through this language. But one must learn to interpret it precisely; otherwise, misinterpretation of body gestures could create lot of problems.

Our body responds to or expresses various emotions like sadness, happiness, excitement, anger, repentance, love, affection, lust, abhorrence etc. You must have observed that when a person is happy or excited over some good happening, his pupils get dilated and cheeks start glowing due to fast blood circulation. Other body parts like arms and legs too develop a rhythm about their movement. On the other hand, when one is angry, the eyes turn a bit reddish, the face is strained and the eyebrows are tightened upwards.

Sometimes, during a chat between two persons, it is observed that one person is the dominant speaker, while the other is a mere listener. Of course, this is not chatting but preaching, in which the dominant speaker is preaching to the other person or instructing him. In such a chat, the dominant speaker can gauge from the expressions of the listener whether the latter is really enjoying listening to him, is a bit intimidated, or feeling bored. For a good conversation, all the participants should have real interest in the talk and they should also listen sincerely to what the fellow participants say. By reading the fellow speaker's expressions, especially facial, one can judge his or her interest. If you see expressions of abhorrence or poor interest on the faces of fellow listeners, check yourself, control your mental faculties, and then go accordingly. Otherwise, such a chat can create unnecessary fuss. It is bad to overload others with your own opinions which they don't want to support. If you persist with such an exercise, then you are simply wasting your own energy.

We humans are social animals and we have to interact with other people in society. During our social interaction, we come across all sorts of people like doctors, advocates, judges, policemen, teachers, parents, colleagues, astrologers, cousins, among others. To interact with all these people in a better way, you must learn to interpret their body gestures. During a court appearance, you can ascertain whether the judge is going to pass judgement in your favour or against by reading his body gestures and the tone of his speech. For advocates, consultants and others who daily interact with their clients and persons from other walks of life, learning to interpret pays a lot. Sometimes during a handshake itself you can judge the nature or intention of the other person.

If a person who has mastered the interpretation of body language tries to fool you, there are still some natural gestures that lay bare his personality, because to hide and utilise all your body is next to impossible. When you are into courtship, there are some gestures of the opposite sex that help you a lot and save you from unnecessary humiliation. Your gestures change according to your mood. Hence learning this special science is very necessary.

I don't consider myself as the most learned guy on body language. Still, I feel confident that my experience in this field can help my readers a lot. After poring through many books written by experts and putting to practice their advice and tips, I decided to give expression to all my experience in the shape of a book. Many books on the subject are available in the market. But most of them are written by foreign authors, hence very few concepts are of help to Indian readers. In our own literature also, modern as well as ancient, we come across all detailed explanations on gesture reading. After developing a fair understanding of these explanations, I have written the present book in which emphasis has been laid to help you interpret the latent meaning behind gestures in the Indian context. Still, there are some common gestures which one sees in use all over the world.

I am sure my readers would really learn and enjoy a lot while reading this book. If you have any problem or query, write to me so that I can help you. Your suggestions regarding this book are always welcome.

—Vinay Mohan Sharma

1

Understanding Body Language

Whenever we talk to or come across someone, either an acquaintance or an unknown person, we communicate with the person through numerous gestures. These gestures reflect our mental state of how we are feeling or observing things. If we are not in a good mood or a little desperate, we become rather irritated and give out defensive gestures. When happy, we feel rather relaxed and active. Our mood predominantly controls most of our body gestures and signals. Even the people we meet try to read our gestures. And, what they think of our personality is reflected through their remarks like, "You are looking smart today," or "Has anything wrong happened" or "Hey! Whom you're going to kill today?" This particular ability to read others' gestures is acquired through experience.

When we call someone perceptive or 'intuitive', we basically refer to his or her ability to read another person's gestures. Women are generally more perceptive than men, perhaps because of the inherent maternal instinct in them, which gives them the ability to understand the non-verbal cues of their children.

There are many genetic, learned and cultural signals through which we communicate with others. Some expressions like smiling, crying, shouting and weeping are considered inborn or genetic signals that we use during different states of mind. These are common in all the primates. Likewise, some gestures like crossing our arms on our chest are also genetic signals.

Still, much confusion prevails regarding the origin of some basic gestures—whether these are genetic or cultural or learned. Like, most men put the coat first on their right arm, while women put it on their left. Similarly, when a man walks in a crowded corridor and passes by a woman, he usually turns his body towards her, while she turns her body away from him.

Basic Communication Gestures

Most of the basic communication gestures are the same all over the world. When we are happy, we smile; when angry, we frown; when sad, we cry and tears roll down our cheeks. When we do not agree with someone, we shake our head from side to side, and we nod while showing our agreement with him. When we do not understand what the other person is saying or talking about, we simply shrug our shoulders in a natural manner. The shoulder shrug is a multiple gesture comprising exposed palms, hunched shoulders and raised brows.

As the spoken language differs from culture to culture and place to place, so do the body gestures. There are many gestures that have different interpretations in different countries or places. For example, the ring gesture, V-sign and the thumbs-up gesture.

The Ring or 'OK' Gesture

The ring or 'OK' gesture was popularised in the USA during the early nineteenth century (see Fig. 1). There are different views about the 'OK' signal. In all English speaking countries, it has the same meaning. There 'OK' implies "all correct" and it has none filtered down to mean 'everything's fine. But in France it also stands for 'Zero' or 'nothing' and in Japan it means 'money'. In some countries 'OK' is an orifice signal, often used to indicate that the man is homosexual.

The V-sign

The V-sign is popular in all Western countries and many other parts of the world. It is a hand sign indicating victory (see Fig. 2). Sir Winston Churchill popularised this gesture

Figure 1—Everything's fine

during World War II. Indian politicians and political aspirants are often photographed showing the V-sign during elections and election rallies.

Figure 2—The Victory Sign

The Thumbs-up Gesture

This gesture has different interpretations across the globe. Hitch-hikers use it for the 'OK' signal. When the thumb is sharply jerked upwards, it means 'up yours' or 'sit on this'. It is an insulting sign. In Greece, the thumbs-up gesture means 'get stuffed'. In India, the thumbs-up gesture is used to communicate varied moods. A thumbs-up sign shared by two friends means 'the going is fine' and between two competitors, the winner uses this gesture to indicate his superiority. School-going and college-going students use it to get a lift.

So, one should be cautious about different meanings of body gestures while travelling in different places. While interpreting the meaning of a particular gesture, it's better if one analyses other gestures of the person, his facial expressions and the very context in which the gesture has been used, before jumping to conclusions.

Power or Prestige Gestures

Research has shown that a person's status or prestige is directly related to the number of gestures he uses. As a general rule, the higher the standing of a person on the socio-economic scale, lesser the body gestures and signals he uses.

The frequency and the type of gestures made depend upon the age of the person. As the person gets older, his gestures become quite refined. For example, when a child of five tells a lie, he covers his mouth immediately with one or both of his hands (see Fig. 3), but when a teenager tells a lie, he simply starts rubbing his finger lightly around his mouth (see Fig. 4). This mouth-covering gesture gets further refined in adulthood. When an adult tells a lie, he simply makes a nose-touching gesture. This gesture is nothing but a sophisticated improvisation of the mouth-covering gesture made by children (see Fig. 5).

Thus, it is rather difficult to detect the lie of an older person through his gestures. Generally, persons who are highly educated and skilled seldom use gestures.

Figure 3—Will I get caught?

Figure 4—Catch me if you can

Figure 5—A seasoned liar

Instead, they prefer verbal communication. Still, one cannot say that it is absolutely correct, for gestures are basically controlled by our brain. This is the reason why one cannot fake body gestures for a long time. But it is good to learn good gestures and get rid of those which give a negative impression about your personality.

OO

2

Gestures and Their Meanings

In daily life we come across various people, hailing from different walks of life, each having a different mood or liking.

We come across doctors, engineers, advocates, labourers, seniors, subordinates, students, relatives, friends etc. While talking with them we do not generally observe their body gestures. Mostly we listen to their talk and believe their words. But when we are participating in a seminar or attending some social gathering, we cannot speak to all persons present there. Mostly, we look at other participants and simply observe what they are doing. We all have different types of relationships with different people, and as per the relationships we do communicate in various ways. In the course of our talk, our body parts also come into action to join our verbal communication.

A person who is not talking also communicates through body language. His body, eyes, face, hands and legs communicate through non-verbal communication, even though he does not use words to communicate and put across his ideas and feelings to anyone. What to believe and what not to believe when a person talks depends on the way that person reacts or communicates. To draw a conclusion about a person's true intention, we have to carefully observe his total gestures along with his verbal communication. This body language can reveal what is there in his mind—whether he is telling a white lie or trying to deceive. There are some obvious gestures, like folded arms, that are associated with a defensive posture.

But there are several gestures which one cannot interpret perfectly, until and unless one studies the concerned person's gestures—that is, gesture cluster. So before drawing conclusions about a person's intentions, we should take note of all his gestures. On the following pages, we are giving details regarding various gestures which are quite common all over the world. The correct interpretation of these gestures will help you read a person like an open book.

∞

3

Palm Gestures—Signals for Understanding

Open Palm Gesture

The open palm gesture has been associated with truth, honesty, allegiance and submission. Many a time oaths are taken with the palm of the hand placed on the chest. When appearing in courts, witnesses take the oath by putting their palm on the holy *Gita* or other sacred books.

Two basic palm positions are generally observed. In the first position, the palm is kept facing upwards towards the sky. In the second one, the palm is facing downwards like a gesture for holding down or stopping someone.

When a person wishes to be open or honest, he will hold one or both his palms out to the other person. When a person wants to open up with someone, he will slowly expose his palms to him. This is a completely unconscious gesture that gives others a feeling that the person with open palms is speaking the truth. A liar has his palms hidden behind his back or in his pocket or in an armfold position, especially when he is being compelled to reveal the truth. His non-verbal communication conveys the impression to others that he is holding back the truth.

Persons who are in sales or similar fields do use this gesture of open palm intentionally to deceive their clients. But an intelligent client/buyer would not get trapped so easily. In fact, when one tells a lie with exposed palms, his other body gestures betray him and he can be easily caught.

'Open palm' gesture is considered to be very good because people showing this gesture seldom lie. Even those who intentionally exhibit this gesture are known to gradually become honest. They find it difficult to lie with exposed palms.

Palm Command Gestures

There are three main palm command gestures:

1. The palm-up position
2. The palm-down position
3. The palm-closed finger-pointed position.

The palm-up gesture is a sign of submission–a sort of request. Opposed to this gesture, the palm-down gesture shows that the request is being given with authority. The person to whom such a request is made feels that he has been given an order. He may also feel antagonistic towards the person making the request in such a way. If both are of equal status, then the former may refuse to follow the so-called request of the latter. But had the request been made with the palm-up gesture, he would have carried it out. Palm-down request is acceptable to subordinates.

When the palm is closed into a fist and the index finger is pointed towards the person to whom a request is being made, it is thought to be browbeating the listener into submission. The pointed finger is rather an irritating gesture. It's better if one avoids the pointed-finger gesture. Instead, we should adopt the palm-up and palm-down positions to have a more positive effect on others. For instance, if you want someone to do a favour for you, or work for you, better use the palm-up gesture while making this request. If the listener is your subordinate, you can use the palm-down gesture. But never ever go for the palm-closed-finger-pointed position.

Handshaking Gestures

Shaking the hand is an old custom. This gesture is used to greet someone or say good-bye. A handshake is a modification of the primitive gesture of both hands raised, indicating 'we are holding no weapons'. Later, the Romans adopted it for greeting. The Roman salute was a hand-to-chest gesture. During the days of the Roman Empire, people used to grasp each other at the forearms instead of the hand. Today's handshake is a gesture of welcome—the interlocking palms signify openness and the touch signifies oneness.

Handshaking customs vary from country to country. Some experts claim to have interpreted the character and attitude of various kinds of people by analysing the nature of their handshake. According to their analysis, perspiring palms indicate nervousness, and the flaccid (dead fish) handshake is considered bad. However, I would advise you not to jump to a quick conclusion about someone's personality by the way he shakes hands. Better to reserve your judgement till you have found solid proof through other means to support your judgement.

When women want to sympathise with or express their sincere feelings to other women, they do not shake hands. They simply hold the other's hands in theirs and communicate their deep sympathy through congruous facial expressions. Remember how Simi Garewal bid farewell to her guests in her chat show *Rendezvous*.

According to body language experts, handshakes transmit three basic attitudes—dominance, submission, and equality.

Dominance is transmitted when a person turns the hand of his partner upwards (to face the sky) and his own downwards (to face the ground) during the handshake.

This palm need not be facing the ground directly but should appear facing downwards in relation to the other man's palm. This type of palm position signifies that the man wants to take control of the encounter (see Fig. 6).

The palm-up gesture shows submission to others. This gesture is just the opposite of the dominant handshake. One offers one's hand with one's palm facing upwards (see Fig. 7). This way you give the other person control, helping him take command of the situation. So it is obvious that

Figure 6—I will take control

dominant persons use aggressive gestures while the submissive go in for submissive gestures. People who make extensive use of their hands in their profession, like doctors,

Figure 7—I give up, buddy

surgeons, artists and musicians, give a limp handshake in order to protect their hand. When two dominant persons shake hands, each of them tries to turn the other's palm into the submissive (palm-up) position. As a result, their handshake is in a vertical position, which transmits a feeling of respect and rapport towards the other.

This particular mode of handshake is popularly known as "Shaking hands like a man" (see Fig. 8).

Figure 8—A manly handshake

When an intelligent person receives a dominant handshake from another person, he does not try to force the latter's palm into the submissive position. But he simply invades the personal space of the dominant person. In such a situation, the intelligent person accepts the handshake and steps forward on his left foot. Then he brings his right foot across and moves into the dominant person's intimate zone, bringing the handshake into a vertical position. To perfect this technique you need lots of practice, because most men are right-footed. Do regular practice to step into a handshake with your left foot and you will find that it is quite simple to face up and reply to a dominant handshake.

Sometimes we come across such situations when we face a dilemma—whether we should go ahead to shake hands or wait for others to come forward to do the same. Many persons who are rather defensive do not come forward to shake hands. While meeting such people, we should wait for their response and it's better not to greet them. A handshake is a sign of welcome, and hence we should see whether we are welcome—if the person whom we are meeting is glad to see us.

Handshake Styles

There are different styles of shaking hands. Some of them we have already discussed. Given below is a detailed account of some more handshake styles.

Palm-down Handshake: This handshake style is considered the most aggressive one, as it provides the receiver of the handshake little time to respond in equal measure. The aggressive type of male always goes in for this handshake, compelling the receiver to do a submissive handshake, as he has to respond with his palm facing up. Still, the receiver can counter the palm-down thrust by following the step-to-the-right technique. But when it is difficult to respond appropriately to the aggressive handshake, then the receiver can simply grasp the other person's hand on top and shake it (see Fig. 9). That way the receiver can occupy the superior position and become the dominant party. This may cause irritation to the person who is quite aggressive in his behaviour, so better be cautious.

Glove Handshake: It is mostly called the politician's hand-shake style. The person initiating such a gesture gives his right hand to his partner to shake and puts his left hand over his partner's hand so as to cover the handshake. His partner's hand is sandwiched between the first person's hands. Through this gesture the person tries to convey the impression to the receiver that he is rather trustworthy and honest. But this style should not be applied to a person whom you have just met as it results in an opposite effect. The receiver may feel suspicious towards the initiator's credentials. Better use this technique with persons whom you know well and want to convince about something (see Fig. 10).

Figure 9—Ease yourself out

Dead Fish Handshake: This style is the most unpopular one, especially when the initiator's or receiver's hand is cold or

Figure 10—Hand in glove, uh?

clammy. It signifies the weak character of the person who makes it. In this handshake style, the hand is held flaccid so that one can easily turn the palm up. This conveys the impression of the rather weak character of that person who is making this handshake (see Fig. 11). Sometimes a person does this handshake unknowingly.

Figure 11—Cold-shouldered handshake

In that case if you are a good friend or acquaintance of that person, tell him which style he should use in future.

The Knuckle Grinder Handshake: This style conveys the impression of a tough man. Of course, one cannot counter it with ease. In this case the only option left to counter it is verbal abuse or a physical action like punching the doer on his face (at your own risk) (see Fig. 12).

Stiff-arm Thrust: This handshake style is mostly adopted by tough guys who are the rather aggressive type and want you to be at a distance and out of their intimate zone (see Fig. 13).

Fingertip Grab: It is like the stiff-arm thrust that has missed the mark and accidentally grabs the other man's fingers.

Figure 12—Tough man's grip

Figure 13—Keeping an arm's length

A person doing so may be quite enthusiastic in his attitude, but actually lacks self-confidence. The main motive of the user of this handshake style is to keep the other man at a distance (see Fig. 14).

Figure 14—Keep off me

Arm-pull Handshake: In this particular mode of handshake, the initiator is thought to be of the insecure type who wants to remain in his own personal space or he may have a small intimate zone and behave normally (see Fig. 15).

Double-handed Handshake: People who want to show sincerity and trust towards the receiver use the double-handed handshake. With one hand (right hand) the initiator shakes the receiver's hand and with his other hand (left hand) he tries to communicate additional feelings. The depth of such feelings is related to the distance to which the initiator's left hand is moved up the receiver's right arm. The elbow-grasp transmits more feelings than the wrist-hold. Similarly, the shoulder-hold transmits more feelings than the upper-arm grip. Besides, the hand shows an invasion of the receiver's intimate and close intimate zones. Generally, the wrist-hold and elbow-grasp styles should be used between two very close relations or friends as in these styles the initiator's left hand invades

Figure 15—I need space

only the receiver's intimate zone. The shoulder-hold and the upper-arm grip may, in fact, involve actual body contact. Hence these should be used only when two persons enjoy an emotional bond. One should never go for using double-handed handshake with strangers, otherwise the person you are meeting for the first time may feel unhappy and become suspicious of the initiator's intentions (see Figs. 16, 17, 18, 19).

Besides the above handshake styles, there are some other styles which we sometimes come across. One such gesture is where the initiator communicates a non-verbal sentence, *"De Taali* (Give a clap)"* and almost strikes his palm downwards on the receiver's palm moving upwards. In such a case, the initiator is always in a dominant position while the receiver is in a submissive one. But one may counter this gesture by invading the initiator's intimate zone. He should also raise his palm to equal height as that of the initiator and make the clap happen in a vertical position.

Sometimes, while shaking hands, the receiver invades the initiator's intimate zone, pulls him towards his side and

Figure 16—The elbow grasp

hugs him tightly. This is seen only between two close friends who are seeing one another after a long time. One should not

Figure 17—The wrist grasp

Figure 18—The shoulder grasp

Figure 19—The upper-arm grasp

go for this gesture with new persons or strangers, as it may make them feel suspicious of one's credentials.

○ ○

4

Eye Signals

Eyes are considered the most important and delicate organs of the human body. Since long we have been describing eyes in different ways as per their appearance. Some of these descriptions are: 'She has beautiful eyes'; 'She has small eyes'; 'He has big baby eyes'; 'He has evil eyes' or 'He looked daggers at him'. When we describe eyes using such phrases, basically we talk about a person's pupils or his gaze behaviour. Eyes may give the most revealing and perfect human communication signals. Our pupils dilate and contract according to different light conditions and the change in mood.

When there is less light or complete darkness, our pupils dilate, while the opposite happens in bright light. When a person is excited, his pupils dilate to four times the normal size. But when one is angry, the pupils contract sharply. The eyes with sharply contracted pupils are termed 'snake-eyes' or 'beady-little eyes'. Romantic encounters mostly take place in dim light as that causes the pupils to dilate. When a woman sees the man she loves, her pupils dilate. Some women use make-up to emphasise their eye display. While into a court-ship, one can easily find out whether his or her partner is really willing to reciprocate by seeing his/her dilated pupils. Young babies and children also have dilated pupils in the company of their parents.

An old saying goes 'Look a person in the eye when you talk to him'. So, when you are negotiating or communicating with others, better look into the pupils, as they can tell you about the feelings of the person. Since long traders, businessmen, prostitutes and gamblers are in the habit of using their eyes to achieve more benefits. The only way to prevent your eyes from betraying your feelings is to cover them with dark glasses.

Gaze Behaviour

When we look a person in the eye and he too does the same, a better and healthy communication is possible. Gazing at others for a considerable time while talking may put them at ease. But if you are angry or profess a philosophy different from the persons you are talking to, your pupils may constrict and, in such a case, a long gaze may have negative results. Still, the length of gaze matters a lot while you are conversing with others. Those who steal their gaze or do not look into the other's eye while conversing are taken as untrustworthy. When your gaze meets the other person's gaze for more than two-thirds of the time of your conversation, it can mean that either you find him interesting or you are simply issuing a non-verbal challenge to him. But in the latter case your pupils would definitely be constricted. In case you find him interesting, your pupils would be rather dilated. It is also observed that if you gaze at a person during most part of your conversation, he may find you interesting and this way better communication is possible.

One should avoid wearing dark or tinted glasses while talking with others as this may make them feel that you are staring at them. But one should not jump to conclusions about a person's intentions by simply measuring the length of his gaze. For, in some countries and places, people do not look at you for a long time. They do not just look into your pupil but also direct their gaze at other body parts.

Allan Pease, the famous writer and scholar, in his book *Body Language*, has given a detailed account of the different types of gazes practised by people. According to him, a triangle can be formed on everybody's forehead. We can construct that imaginary triangle by joining the two pupils and the point between the two eyebrows. This is how Pease's triangle is formed.

While talking with a person, if you keep your gaze directed at Pease's triangle, you create a serious atmosphere and the other person senses that you mean business. Pease has termed this look the 'Business Gaze' (see Fig. 20). Your gaze

Figure 20—The 'business' gaze

should not drop below the level of the other person's eyes, so that you can have better control of the interaction. When your gaze drops below the other man's eye level, a social atmosphere is created (see Fig. 21). When your gaze moves across the two eyes and the chin to other parts of the person's body—to the chest or breasts to crotch—it is termed the intimate gaze, basically used to show interest in the other. This gaze is, of course, for courtship when the encounter is between a man and a woman (see Fig. 22).

When a person uses the sideways glance, it normally communicates either interest or hostility. Sideways glance when linked with raised eyebrows or a smile on the lips communicates interest. And, when it is combined with down-

Figure 21—A 'social' gaze

turned eyebrows, furrowed brows or the corners of the mouth downturned, it communicates hostility.

Some persons who are of the rather irritating type use eye-block gesture. They close their eyelids for a second or longer to wipe off the other person from their mind. In this way, they openly express their disinterest and tell you that

Figure 22—The intimate gaze

they feel bored in your company. When the eye-block gesture is combined with the head tilted backwards, the person is trying to make you feel inferior to him. Of course, this gesture indicates a negative reaction. But a wise man can control the gaze of such a person without saying a word. To do so, he can hold some object, like a pen or something else, between that person's and his own eyes or by making him look at a particular picture or thing.

○ ○

5

Smiling Gestures

According to research conducted by a British team, smiles are of nine types, three of which are very common: simple smile, upper smile, and broad smile. The simple smile with the teeth unexposed is observed when the user is not participating in very outgoing activity. Actually, at that moment the person is smiling to himself. In the upper smile, only the upper teeth (incisors) are exposed. It is often used as a greeting smile. It is usually combined with an eye-to-eye contact between two individuals who are greeting each other by smiling. A broad smile is generally observed to be associated with laughing. In this case, both the upper and lower incisors are exposed but eye-to-eye contact seldom occurs.

Dr Even Grant has defined five types of basic smiles. Of these, the oblong smile finds particular mention. According to Dr Grant, the oblong smile is used when we have to be rather polite. The lips are drawn fully back from both the upper and lower teeth, forming the oblong with the lips. By making this smile, one basically pretends to enjoy a particular talk or joke. But in reality, it does not show the person's interest in the ongoing activity. Another type is the how-do-you-do smile in which we usually expose our upper teeth with our mouth slightly open. In the simple smile, the lips are curved back and up, but they remain together without displaying the teeth. When one is excited and very pleased, one uses the broad smile in which the mouth is open, the lips are curled right back and both the upper and lower incisors are exposed. Another type is the lip-in smile which is mostly used by coy girls. In this particular smile, the lower lip is drawn in-between the teeth.

When there is some conflict between individuals, their facial expressions undergo rapid transformation. Eyebrows are down at the inner ends, the lips are tensed and pushed forward without dental display, the head and the chin are thrust forward while eyes become glaring. In such a situation, the two individuals seldom lose eye contact as that would amount to defeat.

While expressing shock, a person's mouth is wide open and the chin drops. Sometimes a person's mouth is open not because of shock or surprise but because he is trying to concentrate on something very intently. Sometimes, this gesture is also combined with protrusion of the tongue.

○ ○

6

Hand-and-Arm Gestures

Rubbing the palms together is a gesture of positive expectation. When someone is sure of getting money or success in his project, he rubs his palms together. One can see waiters, bearers, and the like rubbing their palms together in front of the customer they have just served. They do this in expectation of some tip or reward. The pace at which one is rubbing the palms is also significant. Rubbing palms at a fast pace shows the person doing this has something good in store for you. But if the rubbing of the palms is done at a slow pace, the good news is for the doer, not you. Rubbing the thumb against the fingertips or against the index finger is commonly a money expectancy gesture, often used by salespersons or the like.

Holding hands clenched is considered a sign of confidence. The persons using this gesture are mostly found to be happy and cheerful. During this gesture, when the fingers appear turning white and seem to be welded together, it signifies a frustrated or hostile attitude—a negative attitude. This gesture has three main positions: hands clenched in front of the face; hands resting on the desk or on the lap when seated; and, hands placed in front of the crotch when standing (see Figs. 23, 24, 25). When the hands are held high, the person doing this is difficult to handle. To counter such a gesture one should do some action so that the person showing this gesture is compelled to unlock his fingers and expose his palm or the frontal body. If you do not succeed

Figure 23—Clenched hands in front of the face

in making the person change his gesture, his hostile attitude remains.

Figure 24—Clenched hands resting on the desk

Figure 25—Frustration revealed through clenched hands

Steepling Hands

Steepling hands gesture is used by people who have a 'know-it-all' attitude or feel quite confident. Senior officials often use this gesture while giving instructions to their subordinates (see Fig. 26). Advocates, managers and the like often use this gesture when they are advising their clients or instructing subordinates. This gesture has two versions—the raised steeple and the lowered steeple gestures. The raised steeple gesture is used by the person who is giving instructions or advice. The lowered steeple gesture is used when the steepler is listening (see Fig. 27). It has been observed that women tend to use the lowered steeple gesture more often as compared to men.

When the raised steeple is used with the head tilted backwards, the performer assumes a tone of arrogance. A steepler having a positive attitude may also make a series of other gestures, like open palms, leaning forward, head up, etc. But when the steepler harbours a negative attitude, her

Figure 26—Know-it-all gesture

gestures may include arm folding, leg crossing, looking away and so on. Thus movements of the person preceding the steeple gesture are the key to its correct interpretation.

Figure 27—Yes, I am listening to you

Gripping Hands, Arms and Wrists

High-ranking officials like the principal of a school or military and police officials, etc. are seen walking with their head up, chin out and one palm gripping the other hand behind their back. This gesture basically signifies superiority and confidence. A person walking in this manner unconsciously exposes his stomach, chest and throat regions to others, which is an act of fearlessness. Adopting such a gesture in stress situations helps a person feel quite relaxed, confident and rather authoritative (see Fig. 28). Similarly, palm-in-palm

Figure 28—Authoritarian gesture

gesture and hand-on-hips show confidence and superiority, but the hand-gripping-wrist gesture indicates frustration and an attempt at self-control. When the hand is moved up the back, it shows that the person is getting more angry (see Fig. 29). One controls one's anger and becomes calm and confident by changing one's gesture to palm-in-palm position.

Displaying Thumb

Thumb gesture displays dominance, superiority, and aggression. But it is considered a positive gesture. When

Figure 29—The upper-arm grip

thumbs appear protruding from a person's frontal as well as back pockets of the trousers, they show his or her dominant attitude (see Fig. 30). Folded arms with thumbs pointing upwards indicate a negative attitude *and* a superior attitude. This is a double gesture (see Fig. 31). One can use his or her thumb to ridicule or disrespect the person standing or sitting in front of oneself by pointing the thumb towards him. Shaking a thumb towards others is generally done to humiliate or ridicule them. Use of this gesture is less common among women (see Fig. 32).

Thumbs-up Gesture

The thumbs-up gesture has different meanings. It is an OK signal, but when the thumb is jerked up fast, it becomes an insult, telling the other person to 'up yours' or 'sit on this' (see Fig. 33). An officer uses this gesture in the presence of his subordinates. One should not use the thumbs-up gesture in front of officers.

Folded Arms Gesture

By folding one or both arms across the chest, we generally make a barrier to block out undesirable elements. When a

Figure 30—Dominant attitude

Figure 31—Superior attitude

Figure 32—Pretty woman, but I can't have my way

person folds his arms firmly on his chest, it gives a strong signal that he feels threatened (see Fig. 34). This gesture

Figure 33—Thumbs-up

44

signifies a nervous, negative or defensive attitude. And when combined with the crossed-legs posture, this gesture

Figure 34—Defensive attitude

indicates that the person is quite tense. In this case, the person communicates his negative thoughts and lesser attention span. Some people may claim that it is a comfortable gesture, but it is not so. Better keep one's legs uncrossed and arms unfolded to be in a relaxed position while listening to others. This body pose communicates, or rather helps, in the development of a positive attitude.

In the standard arm-cross gesture, both the arms are folded together across the chest to avoid unfavourable situations (see Fig. 35). Whenever people feel uncertain and insecure, they adopt this gesture. Whenever you see the arm-cross gesture occurring during a face-to-face encounter, take it for granted that the person making this gesture does not agree with you at all.

Figure 35—Will she or won't she?

As long as he continues with his gesture he keeps harbouring the negative attitude (see Fig. 36). Once he unfolds his arms, he starts agreeing with you. One can control the arm-cross gesture of the listener by giving him some object

Figure 36—Hostility expressed through the fists

like pen, pencil, etc. as that forces him to unfold his arm and come forward. Or simply ask him, "What do you say mister?" or some other questions which will make him speak. Also make your palm visible to the listener, so that he would believe in your sincerity.

If a person makes a full arm-cross gesture combined with clenched fists, it indicates a hostile and defensive attitude. Sometimes this gesture is also combined with clenched teeth and red face, which indicates that the person may attack you physically.

When a person is seen with an arm-cross gesture, his hands tightly gripping the upper arms to reinforce the position and to avoid any attempt to unfold the arms, it is called the arm-gripping gesture. In this gesture the grip is so tight that the fingers and knuckles appear white due to restrained blood circulation. It shows a negative restrained attitude. An arm-fold gesture with both thumbs pointing vertically upwards indicates that the user is a self-confident man but gets a feeling of being extra protected. People who carry firearms or weapons seldom use defensive arm-fold gestures. Police personnel who wear firearms on them, rarely fold their arms, and they normally use the fist-clenched position.

The partial arm-cross gesture in which one arm swings across the body to hold or touch the other arm to form a barrier is often made by a person when he finds himself lacking in self-confidence (see Fig. 37). Another version of the partial arm barrier is holding both hands together, a gesture used by people who stand before the crowd to give a speech or receive some award. This is done to relieve one's emotional insecurity under strained circumstances (see Fig. 38).

Politicians, salesmen, cinema celebrities, etc. who want to hide their nervousness adopt a disguised arm-cross gesture.

In this gesture they simply avoid arms folding, one hand touches a handbag, watch or shirt cuff or is placed near the other arm. In this way, a barrier is formed in front of the body. Some persons are also seen adjusting their clothing or strap

Figure 37—Lacking in self-confidence

Figure 38—Destressing oneself

of the wrist-watch, checking their wallet, rubbing the palms together or doing something that would allow the arms to cross in front of their body. Some people are seen using both their hands to hold a glass of wine or water or the like to hide their nervousness. All this is done to simply form an undetectable arm-barrier in front of their body. Women, particularly, do this quite often. Most of the people use disguised barrier signals in tense situations unconsciously.

○ ○

7

Hand-to-Face Gestures

During the formative years of our childhood, we all are influenced by our parents, grandparents, teachers and other elders. We adopt the body gestures of those who influence us the most. In the process, we learn many hand-to-face gestures, which we use during our normal conversation. However when we see, speak or hear a lie or indulge in some act of deceit, our insecurity is exposed through our gestures. We usually do not attempt an eye-to-eye confrontation. We either touch our mouth, eyes, nose or ears with our hands. But as we grow older, we start using more refined gestures and it is found that our body responds with a hand-to-face gesture while we speak a lie. Studies have shown variations in hand-to-face gestures under different circumstances. A detailed account of these gestures is given below.

Hand Covering the Mouth

To cover up one's deceitful words, one often uses this gesture. In this gesture, the hand covers the mouth partially and the thumb is pressed against the cheek. Sometimes we use our fingers to cover the mouth or use a closed fist. Those who often use this gesture while speaking are liars. But when a listener makes this gesture it simply indicates that he is unable to digest the lie. While speaking to a crowd, if listeners display this gesture, the speaker is able to comprehend that his story has few takers.

Touching the Nose

Basically this gesture is a more sophisticated version of 'hand covering the mouth' gesture. While making this gesture, some people rub below the nose. When a negative thought enters one's mind, a quick response is to cover one's mouth or, in its sophisticated version, to touch one's nose so that it would appear less obvious. Like covering-the-mouth gesture, the nose-touching gesture is used by the speaker to hide his own deceit and by the listener to doubt the speaker's version (see Fig. 39).

Figure 39—I-doubtyou gesture

Rubbing the Eye

This is basically the see-no-evil gesture, through which our brain attempts to block out the deceit, doubt or lie that it perceives. It is also used to avoid having to look at the face of the person to whom one is telling a lie. Women usually rub their eyes less vigorously than men do. They may further avoid looking at the listener if they feel disgusted (see Fig. 40).

Figure 40—See-no-evil gesture

The Ear Rub

This gesture is an attempt by the listener to block the words which he considers a lie by putting the hand around or over the ear (see Fig. 41). Sometimes people who are under

Figure 41—It-is-perhaps-a-lie gesture

immense stress put some objects like pen, pencil or the like in the mouth, which is simply a variation of putting fingers in the mouth (see Fig. 42).

Figure 42—Stressful moments

Scratching the Neck

In this gesture a person scratches the side of his neck or below the ear with his index finger at least five times or more. It is a signal of doubt and uncertainty (see Fig. 43).

Pulling the Collar

Some people unconsciously pull their collar when they tell a lie. In doing so they suspect that they have been caught. This gesture also indicates a person's anger or frustration. In that case the person simply pulls his collar to let cool air circulate around it (see Fig. 44).

Cheek and Chin Gestures

When a listener makes use of his hand to support his head, it clearly indicates that he is feeling quite bored. The degree of the listener's boredom is related to the extent to which his hand and arm are supporting his head (see Fig. 45). The

Figure 43—Signal of uncertainty

Figure 44—A breakdown, reason to be late

Figure 45—When-will-you-shut-up gesture

ultimate boredom occurs when the person falls asleep on the chair itself. Drumming the fingers on the desk or table and continual tapping of the feet on the floor also indicate the impatience of the listener. The speed at which the listener taps the floor or desk, indicates the extent of his impatience. The faster the taps the more impatient he is.

A listener's interest in the speaker's talk is indicated when the listener's closed hand is resting on his cheek and his index finger is pointing upwards (see Fig. 46). The moment the listener's hand starts supporting his head, his interest starts waning. Actual interest lasts till the hand is on the cheek. When the listener's index finger points vertically up the cheek and the thumb supports the chin, it shows that he is feeling negative about the speaker's version. A cautious speaker should immediately react seeing such a gesture by making his talk interesting so that the listener's gesture changes into a positive one. In case the listener starts stroking his chin, it is a signal that he is making a decision (see Fig. 47). If the chin-stroking gesture is followed by crossed arms and

Figure 46—Paying great attention

Figure 47—Making a decision

legs and the listener sits back in his chair, it shows he is not agreeing with the speaker.

The decision-making gestures also vary. People who wear glasses often remove their glasses and put one arm of the frame into their mouth while making a decision. A pipe-smoker will put a pipe into his mouth, instead of using the chin-stroking gesture, when making a decision. When a person starts rubbing the back of his neck with his palm, basically he is telling a lie and hence to avoid the listener's gaze, he looks down. When a person simply slaps the back of the neck first, and then rubs (see Fig. 48) her neck, it indicates that she is

Figure 48—Frustrated

frustrated or angry. Slapping one's forehead signals that the person is not worried or afraid by your indicating his fault. If we try to express this gesture in words, it may be, "Oh no! Not again!" (see Fig. 49).

Leg Barriers

The crossed-leg gesture signifies a negative, rather defensive attitude like the arm-barrier gesture. Crossing the legs is basically an attempt to cover the genital area. One can term

Figure 49—Oh no! Not again!

this pose a feminine gesture as most women generally sit with their legs crossed. One should not interpret the crossed-leg gesture as a defensive gesture in the case of women.

In the normal crossed-leg position, a person crosses one leg over the other, generally the right leg over the left one. In some countries, this gesture is used to show a nervous or defensive attitude, though it may be a supportive gesture if interpreted in isolation. But when the crossed-leg gesture is combined with crossed arms, it shows the doer is no more interested in the ongoing conversation (see Figs. 50, 51).

Leg-Lock Position (American Position)

It is the sitting position used by many persons who have an argumentative or competitive attitude (see Fig. 52). A person in an argument often locks his legs and uses one or both hands with the leg-on-the-top as a clamp. This position shows that he is rather tough-minded and stubborn (see Fig. 53).

Figure 50—Interested in his own affairs

Figure 51—Least-bothered-about-you attitude

Figure 52—Competitive attitude

Figure 53—Stubbornness of the person is
reflected through this gesture

Standing Leg Cross

When an immaculately dressed man stands with his arms and legs crossed and keeps a measurable distance from others at a gathering, it means that he is not well acquainted with the people around him. But when this person stands with his friends, his gestures undergo several changes, like unbuttoning of his coat or jacket, unfolding of arms and legs. He also invades the intimate zone of his friends more often. In the company of his friends, he appears rather relaxed, as his palms are exposed while he leans on one foot with the other pointing towards his friends (see Fig. 54).

Figure 54—Friendly gesture

Ankle-Lock Gesture

The ankle-lock gesture signifies a negative or defensive attitude (see Fig. 55). While males do combine this gesture with clenched fists resting on the knees or with the hands tightly gripping the arms of the chair they are sitting on (see Fig. 56), the females do hold their knees together and the feet may be on one side with hands resting side-by-side or

Figure 55—Defensive attitude

Figure 56—Defensive attitude

one on top of the other resting on the upper legs (see Fig. 57). One can see people showing ankle-lock gestures while in courts, interview halls or during police interrogation.

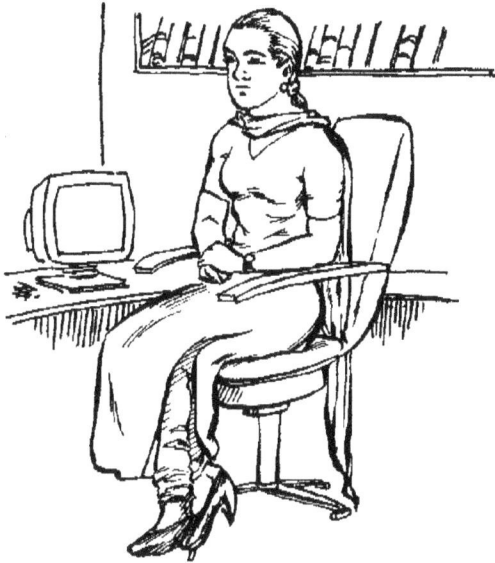

Figure 57—Female defensive gesture

Foot-Lock Gestures

During this gesture the top of one foot locks around the other leg to reinforce a defensive attitude. This position is mostly seen among shy or timid women (see Figs. 58, 59).

Body-Lowering Gestures

When we see someone lowering his body height or bowing in front of a person, it indicates that he is giving full respect to that person. This gesture signifies a relation between a superior person and a subordinate. Most people simply incline their heads or lift their hats, if any, while greeting the other. Even the salute falls in the same category. By lowering one's height or status in front of others who are in a superior position, one can save oneself from many hassles which one often encounters. One can calm an irate customer, a traffic inspector or the like, through body-lowering gestures.

It is important to remember that if you are in your territory, especially your office or home, you will always be in a superior position. And when you go to another's place, his house or office, you will not be in the superior position. But one can

Figure 58—Foot-lock position while standing

Figure 59—Foot-lock position while sitting

show dominance even in the other's house. To do so just go and slouch in an easy-chair and make yourself comfortable in the other's house, while he is still standing.

Some professionals like advocates, CAs and the like usually avoid going to their clients' house or office as this could lower their status and affect their ability to charge the desired fee.

But whenever they do so, they soon accommodate themselves in a superior position through suitable gestures.

○ ○

8

Pointers

Sometimes you may feel that a person with whom you are talking is least interested in your talk and hence wants to leave your company. In such a case, on close observation you will notice that the person has turned his body or swung his feet towards the nearest exit.

Just contrary to this situation, a man who shows interest in the conversation always turns his body towards the person he is listening to. In fact, the physical distance between people is directly related to the degree of intimacy between them. Also, the angle at which people orient their bodies gives many non-verbal clues about their attitudes and relationships. Some of them are described below.

Open Formation

In some countries, people stand with their bodies oriented to form an angle of 90^0 during ordinary social intercourse. When three persons are talking with each other they form a triangle and when a fourth person joins the triangle, all four form a square. Later on, as the number of people increases, they form a circle or two triangles.

Closed Formation

If the angle formed by the torsos of two persons talking to each other decreases from 90^0 down to 0^0, it shows their intimacy. We call the formation so made between two persons the closed formation. When a man wishes to attract a woman, he not only points his body towards her but also reduces the distance between them by invading her intimate zone. If the woman accepts his approach, she orients her torso angle to 0^0 and allows him to enter her territory. This closed formation may also occur between two persons who are hostile to each other. The distance between two persons standing in the closed formation is comparatively less than that of the open formation.

Often a conversation among three persons begins when they are standing in an open triangular formation (see Fig. 60). But in case the two persons keep on having the

Figure 60—You are accepted into the triangle

closed formation position, this gesture indicates that they do not want to include the third person into the on-going conversation. In such a case the two persons will only turn their heads towards the third person without changing the direction of their torsos (see Fig. 61). Such a physical reaction is a clear signal to the third person that his company is undesirable to the other two.

Figure 61—You are not accepted

Body Pointing When Seated

When someone crosses his or her knees towards a person, it indicates his or her interest in that person. If the latter does the same, it shows that he is also interested in the former. Soon a closed formation results between the two that excludes all the others. If a third person wants to participate in the conversation of this duo he would have to move his chair to a position in front of the two and try to form a triangle or do some action to break the closed formation between them. Only then can one easily involve oneself in the conversation of two persons, without disturbing them too much.

Foot Pointing

The feet also serve as pointers and the person towards whom they are pointed is in fact the centre of attraction. When three persons are talking while the fourth is standing as a mute spectator, it is best for the others to point their feet towards the fourth person so that he or she should not feel neglected or bored. If they do so, the fourth person would remain there with the group or else he or she may opt to leave them.

Seated Body Positions

When you want to interrogate or question a person/subordinate, better allow him to sit in front of you on a chair having no arms. In case he belongs to a labour or the like class, you may allow him to sit on a stool also. But you yourself should take a swivel chair with arms to be in a relaxed position. While conducting the interrogation, you can use either of the three main sitting formations:

- Open-triangular formation—when you want the person to have a rapport with you (see Fig. 62).

Figure 62—Open-triangular formation

- Direct-body-point formation—when you want to exert pressure on the person (see Fig. 63).

Figure 63—Exerting pressure on the other

- Sight-angle position—when you want to allow the person to think and act independently, without any non-verbal pressure from your side (see Fig. 64).

Figure 64—Allowing the other person to think independently

○ ○

9

Territorial Gestures

When you lean towards a thing you own or towards a person, it shows that you have a territorial claim over that thing or person. This gesture is also used to show dominance or intimidation when the object you are leaning against belongs to someone else. When someone acquires some new asset like a car, he leans against it, puts his foot on it to show that it belongs to her/him only (see Fig. 65). Lovers hold hands

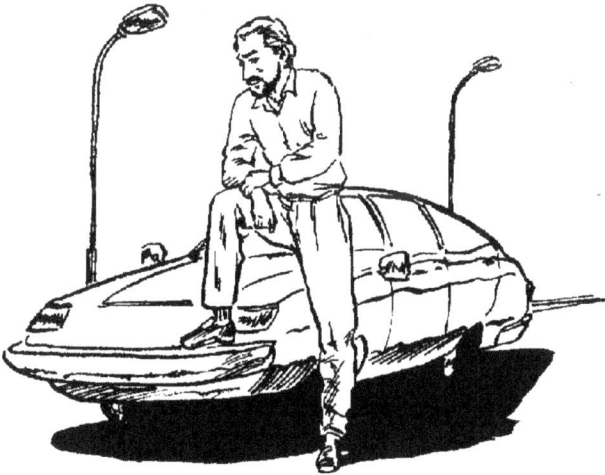

Figure 65—Ownership gesture

or put their arms around each other in public or at social gatherings to announce their intimacy. An easy way to intimidate someone is to lean against, sit upon or use their possessions without seeking their permission.

Some persons are habitual doorway leaners who start intimidating others even on their first introduction (see Fig. 66). Sitting on a chair or seat that does not belong to you

Figure 66—Are you not intimidated?

is also a subtle intimidation technique which can irritate the person to whom the particular chair or seat belongs to.

Ownership Gestures

Ownership gestures are mostly used by persons who hold good positions. Some people use the leg-over-chair gesture to signify the ownership of the particular chair or space (see Fig. 67). Leg-over-chair gesture, if shown by a senior towards his subordinate, shows his lack of concern towards the problem of the latter. Though a person may remain in the leg-over-chair position throughout the conversation, he will probably wear a concerned look on his face to cover up his lack of interest. And when the needy person leaves the place, he will take his leg off the chair and breathe a sigh of relief.

Figure 67—Pride of ownership

If this person, who holds a superior position, is sitting on a chair which has no arms, he may be seen with one or both his feet on the desk. The other subtle versions of the leg-over-chair or feet-on-desk gesture are putting one's foot on the bottom drawer of the desk or placing the foot hard against the leg of the desk to claim ownership of the same. These gestures are quite annoying during an on-going negotiation as they show an indifferent or hostile attitude. Hence, one should take care.

Thinking Alike Gestures

Adopting identical gestures or postures of the person with whom you are talking, indicates similarity in ideas and attitudes between both of you. This is common among people who know each other very well (see Fig. 68). Just the opposite of this situation, strangers avoid adopting similar gestures or positions. Adopting similar gestures is also a way of telling others that you like them. But this gesture should be used carefully. If a clerk adopts the gestures of his manager or

Figure 68—Similarity in ideas and attitudes

boss, the latter may feel intimidated, rather insulted. But this technique is a highly-effective method for non-verbally challenging a person who tries to take control of the situation (see Fig. 69).

Figure 69—Challenging each other

Smoking Gestures

Smoking is an outward manifestation of an inner tension or conflict. It is an attempt by people in today's society to relax. By smoking they just try to cover-up their anxiety. But in similar situations, non-smokers perform other acts such as nail-biting, head scratching, playing with the tie, grooming, finger and foot tapping, etc. The smoking gestures provide important clues to the person's attitude. Pipe smokers are often seen using different rituals, like cleaning, lighting, tapping, filling, packing and puffing with their pipes to make themselves tension free when they are under pressure. They usually take more time in taking a decision in comparison to cigarette smokers. The cigarette-smoking ritual involves tapping, twisting, flicking, waving and other gestures when the smoker is experiencing pressure. One can analyse a smoker's attitude by the direction in which he exhales the smoke. A person with a positive attitude will exhale the smoke in an upward direction, while a person with a negative, secretive and suspicious attitude will blow the smoke down continuously (see Figs. 70, 71). Exhaling down, that too from the corner of

Figure 70—Displaying positive attitude

75

Figure 71—Negative attitude

one's mouth, is an indication of the highly-negative attitude of the smoker. Farther the smoke is exhaled upwards, the more superior or confident the person feels. And, faster the smoke is blown down, more negative the smoker feels. Blowing smoke out through the nostrils indicates a superior or confident attitude, though in this case the smoke is blown downwards because of the physical location of the nostrils. Nose-blowing the smoke with one's head down indicates that the person is very angry. Cigars are a means of displaying superiority as they are big and costly. Cigar-smokers most often exhale the smoke in an upward direction.

Smoking Signals

When we see a smoker tapping a cigar or cigarette end continuously on the ashtray, it shows that he is facing some inner conflict at that moment. Certainly he needs reassurance. When a smoker wants to terminate a conversation, he indicates it by extinguishing his cigar or cigarette without finishing it. When a smoker holds the burning tip of his cigarette towards him and tries to hide it with his palm, it indicates that he does not want to be noticed while smoking. This could be because there are some persons in the surroundings to whom he does not want to reveal that he is a smoker. Such a smoker also blows down the smoke, due to his negative and secretive attitude. Some smokers hold the cigarette or *bidi* between their fingers tightly and inhale the same heavily. Such people either belong to the lower income group or harbour some criminal intent. Through this smoking gesture, they want to show how superior and powerful they are.

Gestures With Glasses

According to Desmond Morris, the act of putting objects against the lip or in the mouth is a momentary attempt by the person to relive the security he experienced as a baby while sucking his mother's breast. Likewise placing one arm of the frame of one's glasses in the mouth is a common gesture, which is essentially a reassurance gesture (see Fig. 72) for

Figure 72—Gaining time to reach a decision

delaying a decision when one is asked to take the same. The act of taking the glasses off at regular intervals, and cleaning the lens is another method used by bespectacled persons to gain time for reaching a decision. If the person puts the glasses back on his eyes, it indicates that he wants to go through the facts once again. But folding the glasses and putting them away is a signal for termination of the conversation.

There is one peculiar gesture made by bespectacled people. It is the peering-over-glasses gesture (see Fig. 73). This gesture is often misinterpreted by persons on the

Figure 73—Peering-over-glasses gesture

receiving end as they may feel as if they are being judged or scrutinised. In response, they may turn rather defensive towards the person who peers over his glasses.

Walking Gestures

Though we all have a particular, rather distinctive walk, our pace, length of stride and posture keeps on changing slightly according to our emotions. When happy, we usually walk quickly and feel rather light on our feet. But when we are distressed, our shoulders droop and we feel rather heavy on our feet. Persons who are goal-oriented walk rapidly swinging their arms freely. Those who habitually keep their hands in their pockets while walking are found to be rather critical and secretive. A person who walks with his hands on his hips is endowed with the quality of attaining his goals quickly taking the shortest possible route. Persons who are preoccupied with some problem assume a specific pose while walking: head down, and hands behind their back. The self-satisfied person walks with his chin raised, arm swinging, and legs a little stiff. Walking a step behind a person shows the walker is subordinate to the person going ahead and is rather loyal and devoted towards him.

Straddling a Chair

Straddling a chair is basically a defensive or protective gesture adopted by dominant and aggressive individuals who try to take control of other people when they feel bored. In case of such persons the chair works as a protective shield against any attack (see Fig. 74).

Figure 74—Being defensive

Head Gestures/Positions

The most widely used head gestures are head nod and head shake. Precisely, the head nod signifies affirmation while head shake means 'no' or rejection.

Head Up Position

It shows a person's neutral attitude (see Fig. 75).

Figure 75—Displaying neutral attitude

Head Tilted to One Side

It shows the listener has developed an interest in the conversation. When one is interested in someone, he or she tilts his or her head and leans forward.

Head Down Position

It signals that the attitude is negative. This gesture is often combined with arms folded on the chest (see Fig. 76).

Hands Behind Head

When one places both hands behind his head, it signifies that he is confident, dominant, rather superior. Professionals like lawyers, managers and the like often make this gesture. Those who feel confident and also argue may combine this gesture with the leg-lock position (see Fig. 77). One can counter such a gesture by copying it.

Figure 76—Negative attitude

Figure 77—Gesture showing superiority

Hands-on-hips Position

This gesture signifies an aggressive male attitude (see Fig. 78). When a person pushes back his coat to his hips

Figure 78—Ready for action

and exposes his chest, he displays a non-verbal gesture of fearlessness. Just the opposite of this gesture, the closed coat readiness shows aggressive frustration. Some professional models (women) perform the hand-on-hips gesture to give the impression that their clothing is for the modern assertive women (see Fig. 79).

Hands-on-knees Gesture While Sitting

This readiness gesture indicates a desire to end an on-going conversation or encounter. This is often combined with leaning forward. The alternative position is leaning forward with both hands gripping the chair (see Figs. 80, 81).

Figure 79—The trendy look gesture

Figure 80—Just getting ready to end a conversation

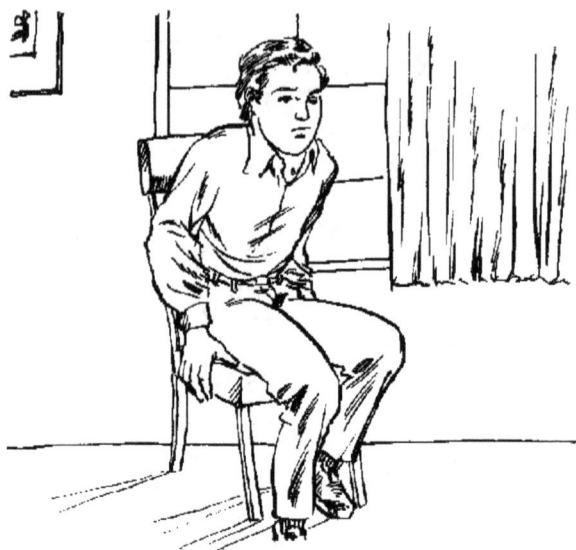

*Figure 81—Alternative position of getting ready
to end a conversation*

10

Territories and Zones

We have seen animals and birds guarding their territories. That's why when you go near an animal, it reacts swiftly. Similarly birds chirp angrily when someone goes near their nests. But if the stranger keeps closing in on their nests, the birds leave the same to protect themselves.

Recent research has shown that men also have their individual territories. As we know, every countrys territory, with well-defined boundaries, is mostly protected by soldiers. Within each country, there are small territories in the form of states, which further have suburbs containing many lanes or streets. A house is also a territory in which we live. A house, in fact, is our personal territory bounded by fences, inside which we keep our things well guarded from others.

Similarly, we have a defined air space around our body, called personal space. In this chapter, the focus of our discussion is this air space (personal space) and how we feel when someone invades it.

Personal Space: The size of the personal space we surround ourselves with, depends upon the density of the population of the place where we have grown up. Of course, city-dwellers carry a smaller personal space around them in comparison to persons coming from the countryside.

Zone Distances: According to Allan Pease the radius of the air bubble (air space) around suburban people can be broken down into four zone distances.

1. Intimate Zone (from 6 to 18 inches): A person guards this zone as his or her personal property. Only close relatives and friends are permitted into it. There is a sub-zone that extends up to 6 inches from the body that can be entered during physical contact only. This we can call close intimate zone.

2. Personal Zone (from 18 to 48 inches): This is the distance we keep from others at social gatherings and parties.

3. Social Zone (from 4 to 12 feet): This is the distance we keep from strangers or persons with whom we have little acquaintance.

4. Public Zone (over 12 feet): This is the comfortable distance from where one can address a large group of people.

Applications of Zone Distances

Whenever our intimate zone is transgressed by another person, it happens due to two reasons. Either the intruder is a close relative or friend or he may be an assailant who wants to attack us. When a stranger enters our intimate zone, he brings about some physiological changes in our body. The heart starts beating faster and the hormone adrenalin is secreted into our bloodstream, which reaches our brain to prepare ourselves for a possible fight or flight as per the situation. When we keep a good distance from another person, we enjoy normalcy. Just the opposite of this situation, when someone puts his arm around our neck, we feel rather irritated.

While travelling in a crowded bus, our personal space (intimate zone) is invaded by others, hence we feel irritated. The same is the case while moving in a crowded lift. Even when we are driving our car and get stuck at a red light, we do feel irritated if some other vehicle is parked very close to our car. So whenever one's personal space is invaded, one feels irritated, unhappy and sometimes very angry.

Here, let us take the example of a large family living in a small apartment. In such a house it is observed that the children's growth is comparatively poor due to lesser personal territory available for each child.

The adrenal glands play an important role in regulating the growth and level of the body's defences. Overcrowding causes a physiological reaction in the form of stress which inhibits normal growth. It has been observed that a city or place with higher density of human population witnesses a higher number of crimes and violence in comparison to places having low population density.

While interrogating criminals, most of the police officers adopt a territorial invasion technique to force criminals to spill the beans. They make the criminal sit on an armless, fixed chair in a room and encroach into his intimate zone, showering him with a volley of questions. In this way, most criminals break down and reveal the truth. Management personnel also adopt such an approach to extract the desired information from subordinates.

○ ○

11

Basic Seating Arrangements

Whenever we visit somebody at his home or office, we are made to sit according to the relationship we have with our host. While in the company of a close friend, we sit with him usually side-by-side or take a corner position but quite near our friend, as this position allows us to have unlimited eye contact and an opportunity to use numerous gestures to communicate with him. In this seating arrangement, we can also observe the other person's gestures well.

Sitting across the table face to face with a person creates a defensive and competitive atmosphere. This arrangement is adopted by people who are either competing with each other or when either of them wants to reprimand the other. The use of this arrangement in an office usually indicates a superior versus subordinate relationship. When a person keeps a measurable distance from the other person, it shows his lack of interest in interacting with the latter. One should not take such a position when open discussion is required.

The shape of the table around which we sit also plays a significant role in shaping different atmospheres of interaction. A square table creates a competitive or defensive relationship between persons of equal status, and such a table is ideal for having short conversations. It has been observed that co-operation or help comes from the person sitting beside you, or on your right side. Resistance comes to you from the person who sits directly opposite you.

Unlike square tables or desks, a round table is used to create an informal, relaxed atmosphere. On a rectangular table, the position (see Fig. below) facing the door, and with the back towards a solid wall with no windows, commands the most influence.

X ▢ Y

If X's back is facing a door, the person sitting on the front position, i.e. Y position, will be the most influential one. Supposing X position is the most influential one, the authority of Y would be next to X. Persons who are of the authoritative type select rectangular tables, while 'open' and 'closed' type of persons go for the 'round' and 'square' shaped tables, respectively.

Power With Chairs

The height of the back of a chair plays a significant role in raising or lowering a person's status. Higher the back of the chair, greater the power and status of the person who sits on it. Also when a person's chair is adjusted higher off the floor than those of others, it signifies the boss's position.

Nowadays, swivel chairs are preferred by senior executives, for they signify more power and status than fixed chairs. Chairs with armrests, leaning back facility and wheels are considered better. Chairs with no armrest, wheels etc. do not signify power and status. Persons sitting on them carry a subordinate status.

How to Raise Your Status

There is a certain arrangement of placing some objects in an office to enhance the status and power of the person who occupies it. Some tips regarding this arrangement are given below:

1. Low chairs or sofas for visitors.
2. A cellphone lying on the table.
3. A telephone placed far from the reach of visitors.

4. An expensive ashtray and imported cigarette container placed out of the visitor's reach.

5. An office wall covered with photos, certificates and awards that the occupant has received.

6. A slim briefcase with a combination lock.

7. A wood coffee table with 2-3 swivel chairs placed at the other end of the office for internal meetings.

8. A glass partition sprayed with mirror finish, allowing the office occupant to see out but not permitting others to look in.

○ ○

12

Understanding Attitudes Through Body Gestures

Boredom

When sitting in the company of your friends or acquaintances, you must observe whether they are really enjoying your talk or actually getting bored. To be termed a bore is not good for one's social standing. But we hardly bother about such reactions, while in an informal situation. A person who is very particular about the listener's interest in his talk never forgets to look for specific gestures that communicate their lack of interest in his talk. In fact, it is up to the speaker whether he wants to bore his audience continuously or, after noticing their lack of interest, change the direction of his talk so that listeners renew their interest. While trying to gauge listeners' interest, you should look for these gestures: beating the table, yawning, placing head in hand, looking somewhere else, putting fingers in one's hair, reading a newspaper, gossiping with others or placing the head down on the table etc. All these gestures indicate boredom.

Sometimes it also happens that a listener is looking in your eyes but actually his mind is lost in some other thoughts far away from your talk. This you can check by simply asking him something related to your talk. In response to your query, the listener who is basically not listening to you, feels perplexed and questions, 'What's that?' Or simply says, 'I beg your pardon'. This clearly indicates that he was not taking interest in your talk.

The 'hand-in-the-palm-of-the-hand' or 'drooping-eyes' position are gestures of boredom shown by a listener who does not bother to hide his feelings.He puts his open hand to the side of his head, drops his chin in a nodding manner, and allows the eyelids to droop, half-covering his eyes.

Researchers say that when a person doodles it shows that his interest is waning. When eye-to-eye contact ceases between two persons, the communication process is jeopardised. Of course, doodling interferes with open communication.

The Blank Stare (Head-in-hand Position): In this position a person is found to be looking into your eyes, so that you feel that he is listening to you. But actually he is sleeping with his eyes open. A more clear-cut sign of disinterest is that his eyes hardly blink. At that time he is supposed to be in a trance, sleeping with eyes open, absolutely hostile or in a state of indifference towards all that is happening. There are many other gestures that indicate extreme boredom, like frequently looking at the wrist-watch, biting nails, throwing one's head backwards to be in a comfortable, rather defensive position. Showing signs of hunger, thirst or being uncomfortable also point to boredom.

Acceptance

How can we gauge that the listener is accepting our idea? To get such an assurance one has to observe some special gestures. During a discussion we often see a person moving closer to the speaker or placing his hand on the speaker's chest or shoulder to assure that whatever he is saying is trustworthy and, of course, the truth. It is very difficult to know whether other people are accepting you, though you can easily learn through their rejection gestures that they have no faith in you.

In a relation like that of husband and wife, one can observe very closely the rejection of one person by the other. When the wife is disgusted with her husband, she overlooks him by keeping herself busy in other petty affairs though her husband wants her company. In such a situation, to keep herself busy she would start arranging things in the room or would read some magazine or some old letter. Or she would just lie down on the bed, with her back towards her husband. When her husband places his hand on her body, she simply ignores it. Of course, in such a situation, she would not talk but would merely send non-verbal signals to indicate her annoyance.

Between two close friends, rejection or non-acceptance is expressed through gestures like touching the other's thigh or placing a finger on his lips or showing his exposed palm, a kind of halt signal. In other relationships also we observe many such rejection gestures.

Now, we come to 'acceptance' of a person's ideas. To signify this 'acceptance', we have some common acceptance gestures as detailed under:

Hand-to-chest Gesture: Through this particular gesture, one endorses from one's heart the other person's spoken language. From ancient times, humans are in the habit of putting their hand to their chest to communicate devotion, honesty and loyalty. This gesture is interpreted differently in different countries. In its various meanings, this gesture indicates greeting others, pledging allegiance to the national flag, openness, sincerity, swearing an oath or making your close one believe your word. But in case of women, it is usually a protective gesture. It may indicate a shock or surprise.

Touching Gestures: By touching, we simply express our emotions to those who are close to us. When someone approaches and touches us, it indicates that the person who has touched us wants us to stop and listen to him. Touching others or grasping the other's hand or shoulder are gestures used to interrupt a talk or put weight on some specific point.

Touching gesture is also used to make others calm. We feel very happy and pleasant when the person, whose company we like the most, showers his affection or love through the touching gesture. Some persons use this gesture to calm the other's excited emotions, while some use it as an interrupting signal.

Sometimes, it happens that a professional is busy giving consultation to his client and his close friend sitting along with him interrupts. If the professional feels bad about his friend's interruption, he simply touches his friend's thigh, signalling him not to do so. Here it is basically an interrupting gesture. It can also be done by simply pressing the other's shoe with one's own. This way things will proceed smoothly and the client sitting in front of them would not notice anything.

Moving Close: If a person moves close to the other, it is viewed as acceptance of the second person by the first one. Actually the moving gesture signifies minimising the gap. To come close physically indicates the person coming close wants to share a thing of common interest with the other person. Sometimes the person with whom one is coming closer to, feels rather uncomfortable by this gesture and backs away. Retreating is basically a rejection gesture. One should always take care of this gesture. Women show this gesture quite often when a man comes close. She may feel uncomfortable and back away, especially if the person coming close is unknown to her. Backing away from a person coming closer indicates rejection as well as becoming rather defensive.

At functions, seminars and parties, the entire gathering breaks off into groups of two or three, where they talk in confidence by putting one's arm on the other's shoulder. This gesture indicates that the person who comes closer or takes another to a secluded place wants to assure him of his devotion, honesty or mutual interest.

Sometimes we come across people who silently and secretly tease another to make him or her aware of his presence at a time when the person so teased is busy talking with others. This may be a mischief as well as an act of stealing the attention of one who is very close to the teaser. In parties and special gatherings, we observe that people who know each other but meet occasionally, simply move closer to converse or greet one another on seeing each other. This shows that moving closer indicates acceptance, at least on part of the person who goes close to the other person.

○ ○

13

Courtship Gestures

All living beings on earth resort to courtship gestures to invite attention from the opposite sex and indicate their desire through different means. For example, frogs croak in the rainy season and dogs gambol around a bitch to steal her attention, so that mating can take place. Lions roar to attract the lioness.

Humans, being the most intelligent of all, have evolved a variety of courtship gestures which they use or receive to attract the opposite sex. As far as taking the initiative is concerned, males are rather bold and rough in comparison to females. Here, I would like to give the example of my friend Anoop, who has developed the skill to attract women. I have often seen him cultivating friendship with a number of young girls, of course, one at a time, during social gatherings. It is not that he has very attractive features, but there is something very special in his personality which makes women drool over him. It is interesting to note that women call Anoop 'sexy'. Men, on the contrary, find him rough, aggressive and proud. As a result, he has very few male friends. The obvious reason is that no male likes a rival when it comes to being an attraction among the girls. It has been observed that females exhibit a greater range of courtship signals in comparison to males.

Dr. Albert E. Scheflen, in his article "Quasi-Courtship Behaviour in Psychotherapy" (*Psychiatry,* August 1965), states:

"People in high courtship readiness are often unaware of it, and conversely, subjects who think they feel very active sexually often do not evidence courtship readiness at all. Courtship readiness is most clearly evidenced by a state of high muscle tone. Sagging disappears, jowling and bagginess around the eyes decreases, the torso becomes more erect, and pot-bellied slumping disappears or decreases."

What Dr. Scheflen has said, one can very well observe at almost all places. On a beach or some garden where people come for walking or jogging, one can often observe a man and a woman approaching each other from a distance. As they are about to cross each other one would also observe some physiological changes taking place, so that their eyes make contact. You can then see that the high muscle tone becomes evident, bags around the eyes decrease, body sagging disappears, chest protrudes, the stomach is automatically pulled in and the body assumes an erect posture so that the person appears to be more youthful. These changes continue until they pass each other. Once they do so their original postures return.

Male Courtship Gestures and Signals

It is a universal phenomenon observed that whenever a lady enters the zone of men, there is a sudden change in the atmosphere. All the men—they may be from any age group—react to her presence. There may be variation in their gestures depending upon their age. Youth express their interest through preening behaviour like straightening their tie (see Fig. 82), brushing dust from their shoulders, adjusting their shirt, coat and other clothing or smoothing their hair. If the man is not wearing a tie, he may adjust the collar of his shirt to attract the attention of the fairer sex.

Those who are rather aggressive towards females display the thumbs-in-belt gesture. An excited youth may turn his body towards the lady and point his foot at her. He uses the intimate gaze and holds her gaze for a longer time than normal. His pupils get dilated, when he stands with his hands on his hips.

Figure 82—Male courtship gesture

Those who are seated may spread their legs to give a crotch display. They tend to straighten their body, push back their shoulders, and often seem too proud to give in and receive the female's positive interest. All these gestures communicate a desire for involvement with the lady.

Perverts do resort to some of the above-mentioned preening gestures. Not only this, they also make some indecent, ugly-looking signals like: showing protruded tongue moving to and fro, moving tongue on the upper lip, showing fist movement and obscene hand gestures, exhibition of pelvic jerk towards the lady, and rubbing on the crotch area while whistling with the lips. These are all vulgar signals, considered an offence in civilised society. And males who perform such vulgar gestures can be prosecuted under the law, if a complaint is filed against them with the proper authorities. Of course, all these signals show the base intentions of the male. This behaviour falls under the category of exhibitionism.

When a man beats his thigh while looking at a particular woman, this gesture indicates his beastly lust towards her.

As mentioned in *Mahabharata,* the greatest epic of Hindus, Duryodhana while in the court, beats his thigh signalling towards Draupadi. This showed his evil intention which was then highly objected to by the Pandavas, specifically the great Bhima. During the Mahabharata war, he avenged this insult by tearing off Duryodhana's very leg from his body.

○ ○

14

Female Courtship Gestures and Signals

Like men, women also use the basic preening gestures, like fondling the hair, adjusting the clothing, putting hands on hips, pointing their body towards the male, extending an intimate gaze, having increased eye contact, checking their nails, etc. Like men, they also observe the thumbs-in-belt gesture. When almost ready for courtship, women undergo various physiological reactions. Their eyes show dilated pupils and the cheeks start glowing. Various other female courtship signals are: turning around and looking in the mirror or glancing sideways to see one's reflection; subtle rolling of the pelvic region; crossing and uncrossing the legs in front of a man; and caressing the inside of the calf, knee, or thigh.

The delicate balancing of a shoe or sandal on the toe of one of her feet is an indication of how comfortable she is in the company of a particular man. When she feels a bit apprehensive or uncomfortable, she quickly puts on her shoe or sandal. Some women communicate their comfort in the company of men whom they like by sitting with one leg tucked under the other. When such a gesture is combined with direct eye contact, it clearly shows that the lady is very much interested in courtship.

Other female courtship signals are as follows:

Rolling Hips

The hips have a specific roll when women walk to highlight the pelvic section. Female models use this gesture to advertise goods and services of various companies. And you may also see damsels using the movement of their hips to steal men's attention. This specific gesture or mode of walking has contributed in identifying some women with a special walking style—*Gajgamini.* A lot has been said and written about women's walk with rolling hips by many eminent poets and epic writers. When a youthful woman walks with her hips rolling sideways, it definitely makes her noticeable to the opposite sex. Seeing this walking style, some men feel as if their heart is throbbing fast. Obviously, while a woman's hips roll, her waist also moves in a rhythmic motion that enhances her sex appeal.

Mouth a Little Open, Wet Lips

The young lady with wet lips gives an open invitation for courtship. Dr. Desmond Morris has described this as 'self-mimicry', for it is intended to symbolise the genital (female) region. Women can wet their lips either by use of their saliva or cosmetics, both give the appearance of sexual invitation. But it also does not mean that the women using this gesture are ultra-modern. In fact, in our society, which is still a bit conservative, women do not use this gesture in the normal course. Women in advertising, modelling or the sex industry do exhibit this gesture very much. Conservative women usually find it obscene and avoid using this gesture, while the outgoing types do not have any qualms in using it. The gesture helps enhance their sensuousness.

Head Toss

One can see this gesture resorted to by women all over the world. In this gesture, women flick their head to toss the hair back over the shoulders or away from the face. Even women having short hair use this gesture in front of men. It clearly shows their interest in that man for courtship.

Open Legs

Among sexually aggressive females, this gesture is widely observed when they are sitting or standing. The legs of a woman are opened wider than normal, if the male is not present around. But sexually defensive women always keep their legs crossed or together.

Sideways Glance

This is in fact the most admirable and pretty gesture used by those women who are interested in courtship (see Fig. 83).

Figure 83—Female sideways glance gesture

This gesture is commonly found all over the world. Actually, interested males do love to take notice of this gesture made by their favourite girls. With partially dropped eyelids, the woman holds the man's gaze just long enough for him to notice, then she quickly looks the other way. This can, of course, light the fire of love in normal men. Some women may try to steal a glance from a handsome person who passed their side by turning their head backwards. This gesture shows their momentary interest in that guy. But it can also lead to a long-lasting friendship, if pursued.

Lipstick/Cylindrical Objects

The use of lipstick is an old technique to mimic the reddened genitals of the sexually aroused woman. When a woman is sexually aroused, her lips, breasts and genitals become larger and reddened as blood circulation increases in these parts on excitement. But one should not always take red lips as a sure sign, for lipsticks are available in all colours. Also, the use of lipstick is no more a European style. It has become common all over the world. It is true that when in a happy mood, women colour their lips. Of course, they do it to steal their partner's attention. Fondling cigarettes, cigars or any cylindrical object is a clear indication from the female's side that she wants to steal the attention of a particular male who has caught her liking.

Female Leg Cross Gestures

It has been observed from various studies conducted in the field of body language that women use a few basic positions of legs to communicate their interest in courtship. One such position is the knee point (see Fig. 84). In this position, one leg

Figure 84—Female knee-point gesture

is tucked under the other and points towards the person who she finds interesting. Here, the woman exposes her thighs to steal the attention of the person whom she considers suitable for courtship. Sometimes, the desirous woman intentionally uncovers her thighs to give a clear-cut signal.

Another position, the shoe-fondle gesture (see Fig. 85) also indicates a relaxed attitude like the knee-point gesture. It has the phallic effect of thrusting the foot in and out of the shoe or sandal, which can make many a man go crazy.

Figure 85—Female shoe-fondle gesture

The leg-twine gesture (see Fig. 86) is the most appealing sitting position a woman can take to express her courting interest. Women, all over the world, use this gesture to attract male attention. According to Dr. Scheflen, in this gesture one leg is pressed firmly against the other to give the appearance of high muscle tone, a condition observed when a person is ready for the sexual act.

Some women cross and uncross the legs in slow motion, in front of their man and gently caress or stroke their thighs with the hand. This indicates their ultimate desire to be touched and fondled. But it is again advisable not to take such gestures for granted. Better to observe other gesture

Figure 86—Female leg-twine gesture

clusters of such women, like their facial expressions, else you will be in a soup.

Though it looks cheap, some women do not hesitate in using gestures like stroking their hips, caressing the lips with the fingers or tucking the thumb into the belt. Some women who wear zipped or buttoned top apparel may even go for unbuttoning or unzipping the same to show their skin. All this indicates their wild desire for courtship. Wearing skin-tight apparel during dates also indicates acceptance of the male for a relationship.

But you cannot say so about all the trendy females who wear trendy clothes. As one swimsuit designer said, "Brevity is the soul of lingerie." Today's designer wear do not leave much to the imagination. They reveal more than they hide. Body-hugging tank tops and jeans are in vogue, hence you cannot say that these MTV-inspired teenagers and young ladies are all available. Apply a little logic and your discretion before entrapping yourself in any relationship.

○ ○

15

Expectancy

When we expect money or some other favours from a person standing in front of us, we automatically resort to some specific gestures to communicate our desire. Of course, we do this when we do not want to make use of verbal communication. Sometimes these non-verbal gestures are supported by a few words.

Described below are some gestures which are supported by a few words and some gestures which are used to express one's desire of seeking some favour.

By rubbing the thumb and index finger together, we communicate expectation of money. This is the most sophisticated way to communicate our desire for money. We see on many occasions watchmen, doormen, bellhops, waiters and other such employees using a variety of expectancy gestures to communicate their message. Verbal language and pauses play an important role in expressing an expectation attitude. A bellboy will politely ask you, "Is everything okay, Sir? I hope you'll enjoy staying with us." After speaking these words, he will stand in the room, waiting for the guest to respond with words or some cash. Similarly, the bearer asks the guest whom he has serve food, "Anything more, Sir? I think you liked the preparations, Sir. Here's the bill, Sir." Then he pauses to receive the cash. Seeing that you have placed some bucks as tip for him, he smiles and gives you a salute with his gleaming eyes and bowed head. This gesture is used commonly by bearers, doormen, chowkidar, (watchman), and the like.

Rubbing of Palms

Rubbing of palms is a way in which many people non-verbally communicate their positive expectancy. The speed at which a person rubs his palms together is a measure of the positive results accruing to the person in front of whom the palms are being rubbed. Fast rubbing indicates good results.

For example, you want to change your present job and go for some good one. For this you visit a placement consultant. After giving you details about some jobs the consultant rubs his palms together quickly and says, "I've got the right job you need." Here, his rubbing of palms gives a clear-cut indication that he expects the results to be to your benefit (see Fig. 87). In case he rubs his palms together

Figure 87—Palm-rubbing gesture

very slowly while telling you about the job, he would then be rather crafty. And, in this case, the expected results would be more to his advantage than yours.

Similarly, a willing buyer would rub his palms together quickly, saying, "Show me something better." This is a clear indication for the salesperson that he is expecting something very good to be shown to him and he is very much likely to purchase the item. But during winter, one must not take this gesture for positive expectancy, for it may be due to cold, as most of us rub our palms together briskly to beat the cold.

Also, take note of this fact that guys in sales are taught to utilise the 'palm-rub gesture' to make prospective buyers feel convinced.

Often youngsters rub their palm together when they see their elders and expect some money from them. Seeing their father with a bagful of things, young ones rub their palms together as they expect something for them in his bag. A contractor who gets a tender for some work will show this by rubbing his palms together, in front of his close ones.

Reading and understanding the palm-rubbing gesture is very important in life. Often people rub their hands together like a washing machine motion prior to understanding an activity. By this gesture they basically communicate their intense interest in the same activity. For example, crapshooters rub the dice between their palms before rolling them. Slowly rubbing wet palms against some cloth communicates nervousness. While making this gesture, men usually use their trousers, whereas women use a hankie or tissue paper. Many persons when nervous, such as a novice making a speech or a witness testifying in court or an interviewee, do resort to the palm-sweat-removal gesture in one form or the other. But before drawing any conclusion you must make sure that this rubbing is not due to itchy palms.

Thumb and Finger Rub

Rubbing the thumb against the index finger or the fingertips is a gesture of money expectancy, often used by sales people. Also, a person who has come to borrow some money would perform this gesture. Sales persons or other such professionals are strictly warned not to make such a gesture as it may make them lose an intelligent buyer.

Crossed Fingers

In this gesture we simply cross the middle finger over the index finger. This gesture is frequently accompanied by the incantation, "I cross my fingers and hope to die, if you ever catch me in another lie." In *Mannerisms of Speech and Gestures,* Dr Sander Feldman has said that this is "a magic gesture, a defence against evil, whether the evil comes from within ourselves or outside". Youngsters perform this gesture while telling a white lie, and also for good luck. Basically the crossed-fingers gesture is made to ward off evil. It has also been observed that people make this gesture during tense situations, when they are making some request or demand. The slightly crossed fingers signify that the person doing so hopes that his wish would be granted. This gesture also signifies "closeness" between two persons. For example, in the United States, the gesture of two fingers held together but not crossed might accompany a statement, "We're as close as that."

Openness

There are many gestures that are part of openness gestures. Some of them are described below:

Open Hands: Open hands show sincerity and openness. Shoulder-shrugging gesture is also accompanied by open hands, and palms pointing upward.

Unbuttoning Coat: Persons who are open or friendly towards others do frequently unbutton their coats or even take off the same in the presence of others. Seated persons unbutton their coats, uncross their legs and move closer to the person they are talking to.

Defensiveness

When someone feels defensive, he or she shows different gestures:

Arms Crossed on Chest: The crossed-arm position indicates defensiveness. This position is used as a protective guard against an anticipated attack. Some persons do resort to the crossed arm gesture whenever they confront their opponents or seniors. Fists reinforce this position. Some people wrap their fingers around their biceps very tightly. This shows their nervous attitude. Women have an upper-torso structure, and they fold their arms quite low on the body (see Fig. 88).

Figure 88—Female crossed arms gesture

Leg Over Arm of Chair: Though this gesture shows that the person is hostile towards the speaker, still some people who are in a senior position use this gesture to show their dominance and superiority.

Straddling a Chair: In this position the back of the chair on which a person is sitting serves as a shield. This gesture mostly occurs during senior/subordinate situations. The person who straddles a chair is least bothered about you and is rather aggressive or of the dominant type.

Crossing Legs: Persons who cross their legs give you the most competition and you need greater attention to deal with them. When this gesture is combined with crossed arms, the situation becomes harder to handle. When a woman crosses her legs and moves her foot in kicking position, it shows that she is feeling very bored with the situation (see Fig. 89).

Figure 89—Foot in kicking position

Evaluating the Listener's Interest: Think of a situation where you are addressing some people. You find a person staring at you with unblinking eyes, his body taut and feet flat on the floor. His overall bearing apparently shows that he is listening to you very carefully. But it is not so; he is least interested in your lecture but pretends to be quite serious while listening to your speech. On the contrary, a person who sits on the edge of his chair, leaning forward with slightly tilted head supported by one hand, is very interested in your lecture.

Hand-to-cheek Gestures: Hand-to-cheek gestures signify a thinker's face who is not only listening to the speaker seriously, but also evaluating his own version. Sometimes there is a slight blinking of the eyes too. Sometimes he brings a hand to his face, puts his chin on the palm and extends his index finger along his cheek, the remaining fingers placed below the mouth. All these gestures come under the critical-evaluation gestures category. When this gesture cluster is associated with the body drawn back from the other individual, the thought patterns go purely critical, rather negative towards the speaker (see Fig. 90).

Figure 90—Critical-evaluation gesture

Head Tilted: This gesture gives the impression of listening with great interest.

Stroking Chin: This gesture signifies that the person doing so is evaluating and thinking continuously to reach a solution to the problem. Once he reaches the decision, he immediately stops stroking his chin (see Fig. 91).

Gestures With Glasses: Dropping eyeglasses into the lower bridge of the nose and peering over them is basically an evaluating gesture that causes a negative emotional reaction in other persons at whom we are peering. These persons feel as if they are being closely scrutinised and looked down upon. Another common gesture associated with spectacles is deliberately taking the glasses off and carefully cleaning their lens, though there is no need to do the same. Another common gesture is removing the glasses from the eyes and

Figure 91—Stroking chin gesture

putting one of its arms into the mouth. This is done simply to gain time. Some persons do throw their glasses on the table while signalling their emotional outbreaks.

Besides the above-mentioned gesture clusters used in evaluation, about pipe smokers resort to specific gestures to gain time to think about the present problem or reconsider their opinions about the same. These actions are—filling the pipe, cleaning it, tapping it, stroking it, etc. Some persons are seen pinching the bridge of their nose while making a decision. This gesture is usually combined with closed eyes. When faced with self-conflict the person may lower his head and pinch the bridge of his nose (see Fig. 92) near the eyebrows.

Suspicion and Secretiveness

All gestures that communicate suspicion, uncertainty, rejection, and doubt carry a common message—negative outlook. The common gestures of rejection cluster are folded arms, moving the body away, crossed legs, head

Figure 92—Self-conflict gesture

tilted forward and the like. The other more subtle gestures include turning the body slightly away and the nose-touching or nose-rubbing gesture. Moreover, the sideways glance and body pointing towards the exit (door) gestures also indicate that the person doing so is in fact feeling negative and wants a quick end to the conversation. Other variations of these gestures are rubbing behind or beside the ear with the index finger and rubbing the eye.

Readiness

Hands on hips is a typical gesture that signifies readiness. The other variations of this gesture are sitting on the edge of a chair, arms spread with hands gripping the edge of the table and sitting on the edge of the chair with one hand just above the knee. All these gestures show readiness of the person.

Reassurance

Clenched hands with the thumbs rubbing against each other is one of the most common gestures, indicating that the user needs reassurance. He is very defensive. Variations of this gesture are cuticle-picking and hand pinching. Another gesture is sticking a pen or pencil into the mouth or chewing a piece of paper. Touching the back of a chair before sitting down on it or bringing the hand to the throat also signify that the person needs reassurance.

The hand-to-throat gesture is seen only in women. Women who wear necklaces can easily disguise this gesture by making others feel that they are simply checking whether the necklace is still there. Women also use a self-pinching gesture when feeling uncomfortable in a particular situation. This gesture of pinching the fleshy part of the hand, communicates a desire for reassurance. Biting nails is also a reassurance seeking gesture.

Co-operation

Sitting on the edge of the chair is a co-operative gesture. Likewise, tilted-head gesture and unbuttoning of coat gesture also fall into the same category. A few hand-to-face or hand-to-head gestures are also co-operative gestures.

Frustration

Removing one's cap, running fingers through the hair, rubbing the back of the neck, clearing imaginary dust, taking short breaths combined with sighing sounds, teeth-cleaning, and the tightly-clenched hands—all these gestures communicate frustration. The hand-wringing gesture is a refined version of the clenched-hands gesture (see Fig. 93). This gesture is mostly observed when someone is being interrogated. When feeling hostile or a bit angry, some persons clench their fists. Some people show the others their clenched fist, but some others hide this gesture by thrusting the fist into their pocket or putting both hands behind the back or tucking both the fists under the armpits in a crossed arm gesture. Fist-clenching is a masculine gesture. Women seldom use it. Charles Darwin has observed in *Expression of Emotion in Man and Animal* that clenched fists communicate determination, anger and a hostile attitude. In *A Manual of Gestures,* Albert M. Bacon has observed that the clenched hand communicates

Figure 93—Hand-wringing gesture

extreme emphasis, fierce determination, desperate resolve or vehement declaration. Some people use pointing-index-finger gesture to reprimand others or for emphasis. Of course, this gesture makes others feel irritated.

Palm-to-back-of-neck gesture communicates emotional displacement. Women disguise this gesture by combining it with a hair-grooming action. Another variation of this gesture is the hot-under-the-collar gesture.

Self-control

When we are angry or tense and understand the gravity of the situation, we try to control our emotions using some gestures. Holding an arm behind the back and clenching one hand tightly while the other hand grips the wrist or arm is one such common self-control gesture (see Fig. 94). Persons who hold back their strong feelings and emotions often assume the locked-ankle and clenched-hands position. When uncomfortable, women lock their ankles in an awkward way (see Fig. 95). Most men are seen using the ankles-locked gesture combined with handsclenched around their pelvic area or gripping the armrests of the chair they are sitting on.

115

Figure 94—Self-control gesture

Women also clench their hands but rest them on their mid-section.

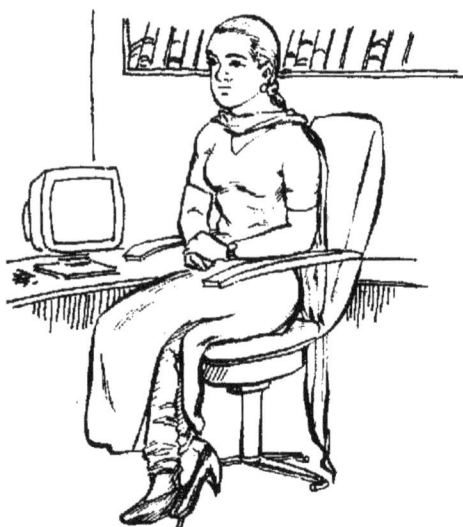

Figure 95—Female locked-ankles gesture

An angry person who feels unable to frankly express his feelings scratches his head or rubs the back of his neck in frustration. He may further go for clenching his fist holding his wrist or arm.

Nervousness

Nervousness is a negative attitude which can be noticed well written on a person's face. Besides the facial expression, there are several other gestures and signals that expose a person's nervousness. When a nervous person joins a conversation, he prefers to sit by crossing his legs and arms, and also pointing his body towards the exit. Persons when anxious or nervous are seen clearing their throat with artificial coughing, whistling or lighting of a cigarette. While smoking such persons prefer to exhale in a downward direction. In a very short time they smoke many cigarettes. In a stressful situation, some persons tend to fidget in their chairs. They also show hands-covering mouth gestures while speaking (see Fig. 96). People who want to hide their conversation consciously cup their hands over their mouths. Sometimes, they put their elbows and hold both hands together in front of their mouth. When faced with a decision-making situation some persons resort to pants-pulling gestures. When feeling concerned about money or the lack of it, some persons jingle money in their pockets.

Confidence

A proud and erect stance is always a clear indication of confidence. Not only is it good for health, it communicates self-assurance. People are advised to square their shoulders and straighten their backs to look more confident. Confident persons frequently continue eye contact with their counterparts and that too for a longer time than those who attempt to conceal or are rather unsure about themselves. Confident persons blink their eyes the least while talking. Gesture clusters that communicate confidence include talking, steepling, hands-joined-together-at-the-back, chin-thrust-upward, feet-on-desk, leaning-back-with-both-hands-supporting head, and cluck-sound gestures.

Figure 96—Hands-covering-mouth gesture

Confident women generally use the covert, lowering and steepling gesture (see Fig. 97). They place their hands on their laps when sitting or join fingers slightly above the belt level. A more subtle form of steepling occurs when some persons join their hands more closely, the arms assuming the basic position of other steepling gestures.

Figure 97—Female steepling gesture

118

Some confident persons who join their hands together at their back, with chin thrusting upward, rock back and forth in their chair with a long back. This is purely a masculine gesture commanding authority. Women seldom perform this gesture because it looks obscene to the beholder. When the hands are clenched much higher upon the back, it indicates timidity.

Gestures that indicate territorial rights, dominance, or superiority indicate the performer's confidence. Actions like throwing one leg over the arm of a chair, pulling a desk drawer out and placing a foot on it, or putting a foot or feet upon a table or chair signify territorial right and communicate dominance and superiority. Leaning against a vehicle or any other object, putting one's arm around the other's waist, or walking hand-in-hand communicates ownership or belonging. Similarly, placing an object like a coat, purse, book or magazine on a desired space communicates territorial rights. One may see persons doing so when they feel like booking a space (seat) for themselves in buses, libraries, parks, restaurants etc. Sitting on a chair and making others stand in front communicates superiority. One can often see a school principal doing this while talking with students in his office. Strangely, cigar-smoking is also considered a status symbol as it is a costly affair. Cigar-smokers always exhale their smoke in an upward direction which communicates their confidence and superiority. Some persons who feel proud make a clucking sound that communicates self-satisfaction. In this gesture the tongue is raised to the roof of the mouth and then it is released to make a sound. Some people make this sound after tasting a delicious meal.

Leaning back with hand placed behind the head is an American gesture. A person making it communicates an attitude of relaxed aggressiveness. Those who assume it say that this gesture allows them to concentrate better on a particular matter which they want to analyse.

○ ○

www.ingramcontent.com/pod-product-compliance
Lightning Source LLC
Chambersburg PA
CBHW060744100426
42813CB00032B/3391/J